# THE
# PINE CONE
# BOOK

# Cones, Christmas and Recollections

# THE PINE CONE BOOK

## Cones, Christmas and Recollections

Nancy Long Boyd

Illustrated by Ellen Oliver Parsons

PROSPECT HILL
Baltimore, Maryland

Published by
PROSPECT HILL
216 Wendover Road
Baltimore, Maryland 21218

Library of Congress Catalog Card Number: 83-62035

ISBN: 0-941526-01-1 (Casebound)

ISBN: 0-941526-02-X (Paperback)

DEDICATION:
To my husband, J. Cookman Boyd, Jr., without whom many of the decorations in this book could not have been made.

ACKNOWLEDGEMENTS:
For thirty-five years I traveled throughout the state of Maryland, to Massachusetts, to several areas of Pennsylvania, to Washington, DC, Delaware, Florida and even to Bermuda lecturing to garden groups about horticulture, Christmas decorations, herbs and table decorations. It was wonderful to meet with kindred spirits everywhere.

In writing *The Pine Cone Book* I have looked back happily over the last forty years of my life, filled as it has been with a wonderful husband, three children, seven grandchildren and several garden clubs. My horticultural interests and my work with flowers and Pine cones have kept me so busy that I have only just begun to realize that I am not as young as I once was. However, I have been working all day today in my garden and still find plants and their wondrous ways fascinating.

My garden club experiences have led me into very pleasant highways and byways. Club members everywhere have contributed to this euphoria. As we worked together in the Roland Park Garden Club over the years for our Christmas Sales, friendships have become more meaningful, a gift to treasure.

I was delighted when two of our club members, Mrs. Fred J. Heldrich, Jr. and Mrs. Roy C. Parsons, invited me to write this book. They have been inspiring to work with, and I am amazed at their excellent understanding of the complicated art of editing and illustrating a book such as this.

Two chapters were contributed—one by my darling sister, Mrs. Daniel Murray Cheston, III, and the other by my charming friend, Mrs. Paul Dibrell Sowell both past presidents of the Roland Park Garden Club, and I am grateful to them for allowing me to include their designs. Look for Mrs. Cheston's delightful small Pine cone tree and Mrs. Sowell's beautiful and unusual wreath.

Please enjoy this book with me!

Nancy Long Boyd
Baltimore, Maryland
May, 1983

# Recollections

In the midst of a heavy snowstorm this past winter my youngest granddaughter burst into my house waving a Norway Spruce cone, one of dozens dislodged by the storm.

What is this strange thing, said her wide-eyed two-year old expression.

Ah! A chip off the old block, thought I, and cast around in my cone-filled memory for a way to explain that the treasure she had found was a seed pod from one of those big evergreen trees standing between us and our neighbors.

When she had run off, I thought back over the years to the days when my own three children used to scour the neighborhood to find Spruce cones, Horse Chestnuts, large and small Acorns, Sweet Gum balls, Wisteria pods, or any of hundreds of nature's delightful and intricate miracles that I have always loved. They still bring me gifts of cones and pods, nuts and flowers.

A lifelong interest in cone collecting and plant experimentation is a direct inheritance from my mother's side of the family which had its roots deep in the soil of both Southern and Northern England. As far back as we have been able to trace, there was always a greenhouse, gardens or a plant room as part of the family's life.

My formal education in horticulture began shortly after my marriage in 1934 when I went back to the Johns Hopkins University to take a Ph.D. in Botany. I completed one year and then my professor died. The university was undergoing a general overhaul at that time and it was decided not to replace the Botany professor. This ended my studies at Hopkins. I would have transferred to another institution except that by then I had a small child and my time was not my own. When this happy event became multiplied by three, I gave up the Ph.D. idea, but never the interest in plants of all kinds.

Meantime I became chairman of this garden group or that and, when faced with a last-minute speaker's cancellation on one occasion, I was forced to prepare and deliver my own lecture for the program. This I continued to do for thirty-five years in any weather, all over Maryland and in other states as well. Everywhere I went I inquired of the people I came across what sorts of trees grew in their area and then begged, borrowed, or stole any cones or pods I found.

Also, my mother had a home in St. Petersburg, Florida, and a poodle who needed to be walked. He and I both enjoyed exploring all the back alleys in the neighborhood, often returning home with an almost unmanageable haul of Palm spathes, Pine cones, unusual branches, plants, even shells. Happily, these fascinating treasures could all be stashed in the car and brought back to Maryland.

I am also a dedicated beachcomber, not only in the area of the water's edge, but also in the dunes which harbor water-washed wood, dried starfish, bits of bright-colored nylon rope and old lobster pots. You can imagine what my basement looks like! Most of this flotsam and jetsam has been stashed away helter-skelter down there, but finally I have learned to keep different varieties of cones and pods in separate bags or boxes, thus making it easier to create wreaths and other displays without too much hunting and picking. It is a good idea to separate large and small cones of the same variety, too, as another time-saver. I long ago discovered that my attic attracts squirrels and mice, so nothing is stored there.

I also love the woods where I find all sorts of mushrooms, interesting bits of wood, dried flowers and mosses, particularly the green velvet buttons which are called *Leucobryum glaucum*. These are attractive in what my mother called "Japanese dish gardens." Unusual stones are useful, too.

# Gathering Cones, Pods and Nuts

*Fir Up*

*Spruce Down*

In addition to my preoccupation with gathering all sorts of pods and nuts, I have, over the years, become dedicated to protecting and preserving all the endangered native plants placed on conservation lists in various parts of the country. I truly wish all gardeners in our vast land would learn to recognize these plants and protect them. Every state has a somewhat different list so, as you travel, ask before you pick.

In the field of Botany it is necessary to group plants into families, and the family which contains Pine, Spruce, Hemlock, Larch and Fir is called Pinaceàe, but the seed cases of all these varieties are commonly called Pine cones. This group of trees is known as conifers and all are evergreen, so throughout the book I am using the expression Pine cone in a generic manner.

It may come as a surprise to new gardeners that not all needled evergreens bear cones. Yew, for instance, has plump red berries with a hard seed, a drupe, inside. Do not eat them as they are toxic! Juniper has spicy-tasting black berries, used to flavor a variety of gin.

It is fun to be able to identify these fascinating and varied seed pods. For instance, the cones of Spruce and Fir look much alike, until you see them growing on trees. Fir cones are always upright, like soldiers. Spruce cones hang down. The word Spruce has more letters than Fir, and the word down has more letters than up, so Spruce and down go together, as do Fir and up. Now you can tell which is which at a glance!

The more you study and collect conifers and their seeds, the more aware you will become of the many other plants that produce fascinating and beautiful seeds and seed cases, all of which can be gathered for decorative use.

If you are planning to make your own wreaths and garlands you must begin looking for interesting things to use in late Summer or early Fall. If you take regular walks, remember where the nut trees are, or the Magnolia for its pods, the White Pine for its cones. When you travel, remember that deserts have interesting things, as do the mountains and the seashore. If you vacation in the woods, do not forget to note lichens, Beech nuts, interesting Pine cones or sturdy grasses.

The following lists may provide a start for your collecting, but remember that my lists, since I am a Marylander, are oriented toward what is available on the East Coast, with the addition of items that are generally available at florist supply houses.

Pine cones should be gathered when they are mature, but still bright of color and in perfect condition. If you can pluck them from the tree, so much the better. The longer they lie on the ground the less attractive they become. Look for them after windstorms beginning in the Spring, but early Fall is peak time for a cone harvest.

Cones can be heated in a warm oven, 150° to 200°, for twenty minutes to kill insects and melt resin.

Some long cones such as the Eastern White Pine and Norway Spruce can be split in half by cutting up from the bottom of the stem about 1/2 inch, putting your fingers into the cut and pulling the halves apart.

White Pine cones can also be cut crosswise with sturdy clippers to make attractive cone "flowers" that look a bit like Daisies. Spruce cones can be cut this way too, but the slices are smaller and look more like Cosmos. Other cones are so hard that it is impossible to cut them by hand. For these a band saw is needed. Large Loblolly Pine cones and Sugar Pine cones are like this, but their slices are quite handsome when they are available and perfect for use in focal points.

### Cones

| | |
|---|---|
| Casuarina | Pinyon Pine |
| Deodar Cedar | Pitch Pine |
| Balsam Fir | Ponderosa Pine |
| Douglas Fir | Red Pine |
| Noble Fir | Sand Pine |
| Silver Fir | Scotch Pine |
| Hemlock | Shortleaf Pine |
| Austrian Pine | Virginia Pine |
| Black Pine | Western White |
| Eastern White | Pine |
| Pine | Yellow Pine |
| Jack Pine | Blue Spruce |
| Jeffrey Pine | Norway Spruce |
| Loblolly Pine | Red Spruce |
| Longleaf Pine | Sitka Spruce |
| Marsh Pine | White Spruce |

All kinds of nuts, seeds, dried pods, empty seed containers and even dried leaves and flowers are attractive and usable. They add texture and color not available in cones. Sometimes, in order to wire them, a hole can be made with a sharp needle or an ice pick, but usually a drill will be needed.

The easiest way to drill nuts and pods is to use an electric drill on a stand that allows it to be lowered to the work. An electric drill can be purchased for a very reasonable price and, properly cared for, will last for years. There are hand drills which are less expensive, but they are not as easy to use.

Whether you are working with a hand or electric drill it is a good idea to make a holding device so you can steady the nuts or pods while you drill them. To make a holder use a small piece of wood 1-1/2 to 2 inches thick and gouge out several sizes of holes to fit different sizes of nuts or pods. The pods can then be placed inside the holes and held steady for drilling.

Once a hole has been drilled, a wire stem can be inserted so the nut or pod can be used in any kind of design. Be sure to cover all wires that might show with brown floral tape twisted down and around the wires.

## Pods and Nuts

Acorns
Apricot pits
Avocado seeds
Beech nuts
Beech nut burrs
Brazil nuts
Chestnuts
Chestnut burrs
Coconut seeds
Cotton pods
Day Lily pods
Dried artichokes
Eucalyptus pods
Fern spore cases
Gourds
Haole ribbons
Hazel nuts
Hickory nuts
Jacaranda pods
Kentucky Coffee
  beans
Lichens and fungi
Lotus pods
Magnolia pods
Milkweed pods
Okra pods
Peach pits
Pecans
Persimmon calyx
Persimmon seeds
Pistachio nuts
Poppy pods
Protea flowers
Siberian Iris pods
Sterculia pods
Strawberry corn
Sweet Gum balls
Teasles
Tulip tree pods
Wisteria seeds
Wisteria pods
Yucca pods

## Equipment

Brown felt
Clear spray shellac
A drill, electric is best
Floral clay
Florist pole pins
Florist picks
Gold spray paint
Glycerine
Green and brown florist tape.
  Always store this tape in a
  plastic bag so it does not dry
Hardware cloth, 1/2-inch mesh
Jigsaw
Masonite, 1/4-inch thick
Plaster
Spray paint for styrofoam
Velvet leaves
White craft glue
Wire cutters
#24 florist wire

Florist Pick     Holder for Drilling Nuts     Pole Pin     Hardware Cloth     Wire Cutter

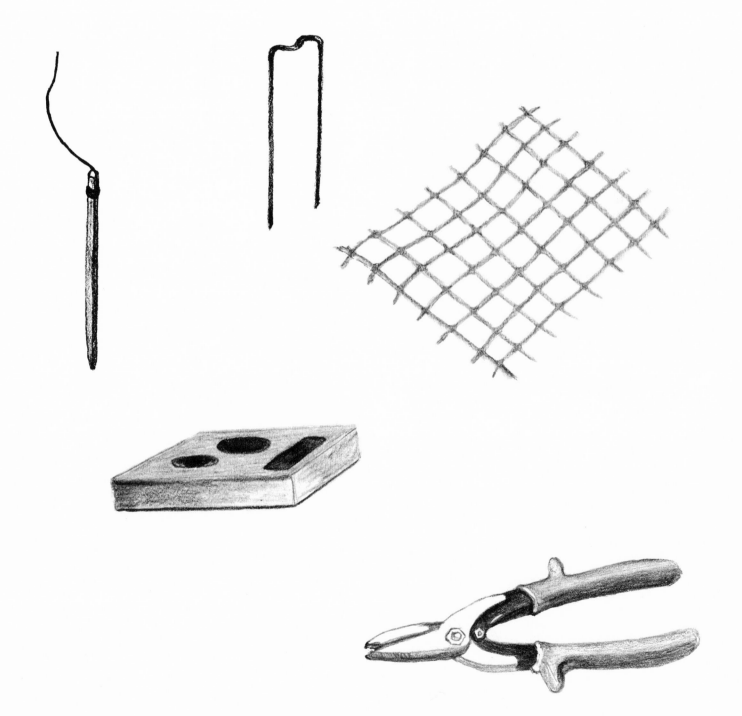

# Evergreens

Nearly all of us who garden have some form of evergreen tree or shrub on our property. Wait until the Holidays to prune them and use the cuttings where they are needed. Except for the Hemlocks, most of them do not go to pieces quickly.

When you cut evergreens put them in deep water at once and they will keep much longer. If you put 2 tablespoons of glycerine in a container holding a gallon of water they will last even longer.

Blue Cedar, *Cedrus Atlanticus glauca*, has handsome pendulous branches with egg-shaped cones lovely on a mantel shelf and in arrangements.

Cedar of Lebanon, *Cedrus lebanotica*, has beautiful deep green needles with cones which are shorter and plumper than Blue Cedar.

Red Cedar is usually found where lime is prevalent. It is really a Juniper, *Juniperus virginiana*.

Douglas Fir, *Pseudotsuga taxifolia*, is good for making an attractive frame around Pine cone wreaths. The cone from this tree has an extra scale which looks as if it is sticking its tongue out.

Noble Fir is a native of Oregon and is a lovely tree to own because it does not shed its needles! Its botanical name is *Abies Nordmanniana* and it is lovely on a mantel, in a wreath, a swag, anywhere. Put this evergreen away carefully in a plastic bag in the attic to be used another year. It will turn a pretty golden brown color and can be used that way or sprayed gold. The gold color will last one year and then it will need to be sprayed again as the gold will turn dark.

Hemlock, *Tsuga canadensis,* can be found growing in the suburbs everywhere in the East. Landscapers fifty years ago used them extensively because they are so successful planted as a screen from neighbors or from unwanted views. Never, but never, use it in the house! It rapidly loses its needles in the warmth, becoming unsightly and making trouble for the housewife. Better leave it outside to do its job as a screen. Its small cones, however, are quite useful in making wreaths of all sizes.

Norfolk Island Pine is *Araucaria excelsa.* I have a handsome one in my plant room. One year I used it for our Christmas tree, but the branches of this lovely tree were not sturdy enough to support anything heavy. If all the decorations had been paper, it would have been fine. Now I am waiting to see what it will do when it is older and stronger.

Pine of all sorts reminds us of the Holidays all year round. There are thirty-four or more varieties in our area; all are attractive wherever used. They are long-leaved, or long-needled, and have fascinating and different cones which are wonderful for decorative use. They carry their cones both hanging down and standing up, but their long needles will distinguish them from Fir and Spruce.

Holly, *Ilex*, is a really Christmassy evergreen with its pretty red berries but, unhappily, it dries out very fast and both leaves and berries fall. The dry leaves are very stickery to pick up by hand. If you use holly, spray it with a preservative before arranging.

Magnolia is handsome used in many ways, but it lasts longer if it is glycerinized so that the leaves remain supple on the branches. To glycerinize leaves, cut fresh branches of Magnolia. Magnolia bought from the florist has already been cut for too long to be able to draw water or glycerine up into its leaves. Put fresh branches into a tall narrow container, but first pound the ends of the branches with a hammer so the glycerine can be absorbed. Put 1/3 cup of glycerine into the container, then add 1 cup of water. Allow the Magnolia to remain in the glycerine and water until you can feel the glycerine on the underside of the tallest leaves. They turn a warm golden brown color. If these branches are protected after use by being stored in a plastic bag, they will be attractive for several years. Leucothoe also glycerinizes well. It turns a deep red.

English Boxwood, *Buxus,* is lovely and long-lasting.

*Arborvitae thuga,* which has scales rather than needles, comes in yellow, mahogany red and bright green. This evergreen looks well when cut and bunched together.

*Yew* of all varieties lasts well in water but it needs to be displayed against a brighter green evergreen as its needles are dense and dark.

Eucalyptus foliage is used glycerinized or dried. It comes in a lovely blue-green or a deep mahogany red. Both of these colors set off Pine cones to great advantage.

Spanish moss, which is found festooning trees from South Carolina to Florida, can be used in a variety of ways at Christmas. It makes a lovely airy wreath when wrapped around a styrofoam ring and held in place with smearings of white craft glue. Use pole pins to secure it to a wire wreath form which has been stuffed with Sphagnum moss. The plant is called *Tillandsia* and is a member of the Bromeliad group. It can be used to make charming birds' nests of any size.

For stylized and exotic effects, Palmetto and Palm fronds can be quite effective. Also try using Yucca's spear-like leaves tied in knots and allowed to veer off in interesting directions. When dry the knotted leaves can be sprayed gold.

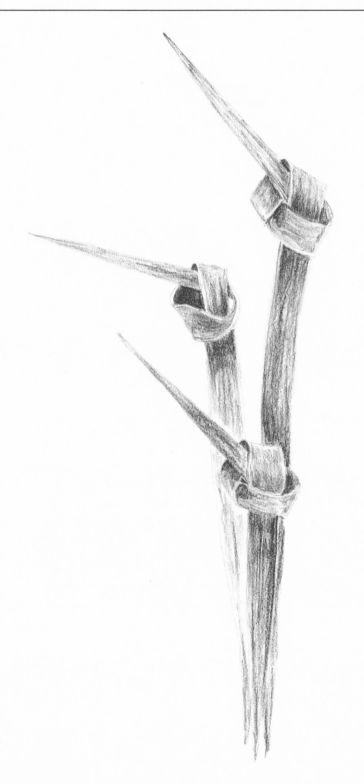

# Pinaceae Family

*White Pine*                    *Canadian Hemlock*

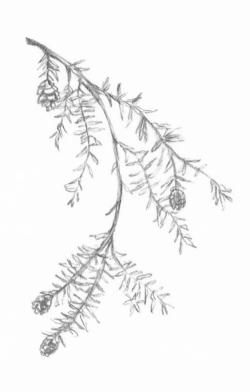

# Masonite Wreath Rings

Probably the most traditional way to decorate a front door for Christmas is with a wreath. The size of the wreath should be dictated by the size of the door, and the style of decoration by the architectural style of the house. For instance, a colonial house looks best with all natural cones and fresh evergreens; a modern house, like modern art, allows your imagination to run riot!

I can't remember how many years ago I made my first cone wreath, but I am sure that the ones I helped my mother make were, like the ones I make today, on a Masonite base. Hers were cut for her by her chauffeur-gardener who was very good at making whatever unusual object she dreamed up. My father was a building contractor, but not the kind who could even drive a nail.

I am lucky enough to have a husband who loves to use all sorts of tools, hand or electric, and who is willing to make anything I want. I know that today many women can also work with these tools, but unhappily I am all thumbs, so when it became obvious that in writing this book I would have to describe some of the constructions, including cutting wreath bases, I persuaded my husband to help. The following directions for making Masonite wreath rings are largely his.

In back of every successful wreath is the base on which it is built. Whatever size wreath is desired, the base should be of rigid material. Plywood or one of the composition boards, such as Masonite, is recommended because wood has a tendency to splinter. The best thickness to use is 1/4 inch. Thinner board is likely to buckle when the decorations are wired onto it.

For a standard 14-inch wreath you will need to start with a piece of board about 15 inches square. Fix the center of the square by drawing lines between opposite corners.

Circles can be drawn in a number of ways—with a compass, for instance, or using a pencil and a piece of wire. If you plan to cut many wooden rings of the same size, a helpful guide can be made using a thin 12-inch wooden ruler. Actually, any thin piece of wood about 12 inches long will do, but the ruler is better because it is marked.

Start by drilling a hole through the ruler at the 1-inch mark. It is easier to put the hole there, rather than at a mark nearer the end. Wherever you start, for a 14-inch wreath, drill another hole 7 inches from the first hole because a 7-inch radius will produce a 14-inch diameter.

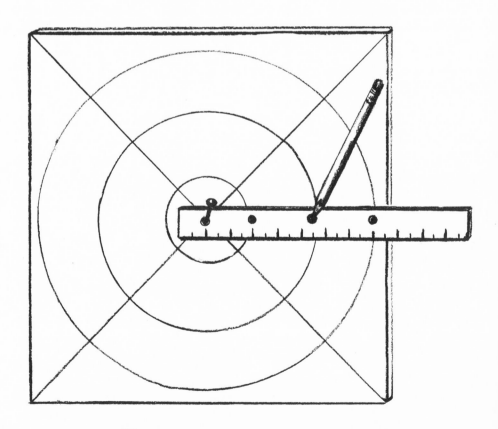

20

Now you must work backwards to establish the widths of the wreath rings you wish to produce. To make the ring 2-1/2 inches wide, the next hole should be drilled 4-1/2 inches from the centering hole on the ruler. This will describe a circle with a diameter of 9 inches.

You can use the remaining inside circle as a solid plaque, or make a second smaller wreath base. If the latter, drill another hole 2 inches from the center hole. This will allow a rim of 2-1/2 inches for the smaller wreath base, also.

The remaining 4-inch circle of Masonite will make a usable bobeche base if a hole large enough to accept a candle is cut in the middle.

Now drive a nail into the center of the square of Masonite and slip the centering hole of the ruler over the nail. By inserting a pencil into each succeeding hole, the necessary series of circles can be drawn.

To cut the wreath forms you could use a hand-held jigsaw, but a stand-up jigsaw is much to be preferred. With either tool, however, the inner circles require a bit of special attention.

The first or outside circle can be cut by simply sawing in from the edge of the square and proceeding around until the circle is completed. To start cutting the next circle, however, a hole large enough to accept the width of the jigsaw blade must be drilled on the inside line. Then the blade can be inserted and the next circle cut. Repeat this process with all the succeeding marked circles.

Depending on the strength of the jigsaw, you may be able to cut out more than one set of rings at a time. To do so, several thicknesses of Masonite must be nailed together. Gain a little experience before you try this maneuver.

Unless you are good with tools you will find these circles are not easy to make. If they do not turn out to be perfect circles, do not worry. You will compensate for this with the cones covering the form.

As an alternative to making your own wreath bases, you may have a hardware store in your neighborhood whose owner will cut out the wreath bases for a price or you might try a friendly lumber yard.

In any case, the edges of the wreath forms will need to be sanded.

Finally, the surface of the wreath bases must be completely dotted with holes. Before boring these holes, place an old board under the Masonite to inhibit blistering. Some sanding may still be necessary to clear the holes.

Using a 3/32-inch drill bit, make an outermost circle of holes around the edge of the ring 1/2 inch in from the rim, about 3/4 inch apart. Drill holes over the remaining surface of the ring 3/4 inch apart.

Two things remain to be done before the decorating begins. A brown felt backing should be cut to fit the wreath form and a sturdy wire hanger should be made and inserted in the frame somewhere near the outside rim. A small ribbon tied to the hanger will make it easy to find when the back of the wreath is a tangle of wires.

Wiring a cone is the same no matter what size cone is used. Try not to cut the piece of wire too long for the cone. It takes a lot of wire to make a wreath and wire is not cheap, even wholesale. Large cones require 8-inch wires, medium cones need 6-inch ones and small cones about a 4-inch length.

Cut a handful of wires to suit the size of your cones. Fold each wire in half and fit it around a row of scales near the bottom of the cone. Twist the wire together once. Repeat for the opposite side so each cone will have two wires attached.

To fix the cone to the wreath base thread each set of wire ends through two adjacent holes in the Masonite. Then twist these ends together in the back and push them as flat as possible.

The preceding directions can be used for wiring cones to any kind of wooden base. Our club makes a lot of 9-inch wreaths to be used on individual apartment doors. These smaller wreaths look best if small cones are used, with perhaps a single focal point of somewhat larger cones and pods.

When making bobeches with the very small Masonite rings, we use the smallest cones such as Hemlock or Larch. Since a bobeche cannot be expected to outlast many candles, we glue the cones onto these bases.

Many people who make cone wreaths use the modern glue gun. I have worked with cones for many years and I still feel that the best way to secure cones is to wire them. Too often wreaths carefully put away for the summer emerge just before Christmas minus many cones which have fallen off when the glue dried. The residue of glue is almost impossible to remove and bumps of it here and there are always just where you need to drill a hole to make repairs.

Begin to decorate a Masonite wreath base by wiring cones around the outside edge. Since these will act as a frame for the picture being created, try to select short flat-bottom cones of the same size, color and variety. Fix the cones as firmly as possible to the outside rim of the wreath, using the row of holes drilled around the circumference of the Masonite. Each cone should be pushed into its neighbor, scales intermingled. When the circle is complete, the cones should not wobble. The inner edge of the wreath is not treated in the same manner. It is only necessary that no Masonite shows when the wreath is finished.

## Wiring Cones Around the Outside Edge of a Masonite Wreath

*Front View, holes enlarged to show detail*

*Whole View, front*

*Back View*

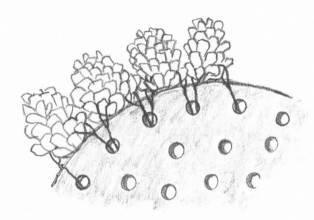

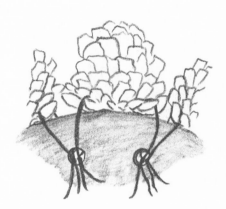

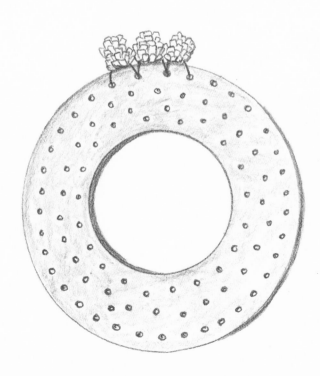

23

Start the wreath design by mentally dividing the frame into sections, either halves, thirds or quarters. These sections are then decorated in a similar manner, which reinforces the design.

Many cones of different kinds will be needed. Look for cones with unusual shapes and colors. Weathered gray cones, however, are not very attractive except, perhaps, for contrast. Torn and battered cones are not attractive either. Some, such as the Eastern White Pine cones, can be used in the form of slices which look like open flower faces. Others can be wired to show their interesting stem formation. All should be chosen for perfection of scales and quality of color.

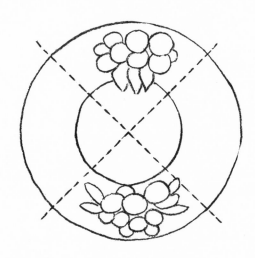

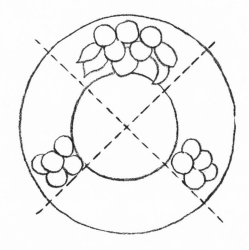

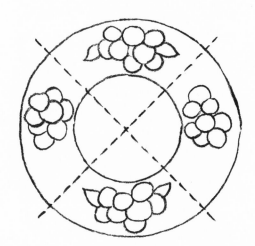

Nature has provided seeds and pods of every size, shape and variety, regardless of where we live. If your state has one kind of cone or pod, but not another, perhaps you can arrange to trade with a friend in another part of the country.

Beautiful Pinyon Pine cones from the Southwest are a pale honey color and look like wooden Chrysanthemums. Eucalyptus pods from California come in many different sizes, shapes and colors and add a distinctive charm to any wreath, as do Jacaranda seed pods which can be used whole or split into halves.

Partially opened Hickory nuts, the outside covering just beginning to split open, are interesting and so are Sweet Gum balls. The latter can be used as a frame on small wreaths, as can the outside husks of Beech nuts.

Acorns of all types are appealing. Especially endearing are the large Acorns with fringed cups which come from the Burr or Mossy Cup Oak. The nut will need to be removed from the cup, the cup drilled across and wired, and then the nut glued back inside.

Wisteria seeds, drilled and wired in a bunch, are charming, as are their outside overcoats. Use anything interesting and long lasting that nature has provided. Just be sure it does not shatter when gently squeezed in your hand.

Very small nuts and pods are useful for filling in the spaces remaining between the larger cones in your design.

25

When all of the wreath is covered with cones and all the wires flattened on the back, glue on the brown felt backing with white craft glue.

To protect the finished wreath from dust and dirt and to make it bright and shiny, spray a clear lacquer over the entire surface. Clear spray comes two ways, thick and thin. The thicker spray will last longer and give greater protection to fragile tips and edges but it may add a pearly, somewhat opaque, glaze to the surface of the cones. The thinner spray will need to be applied three or four times.

After you have finished your nut and cone wreath and are ready to hang it on the front door you may decide it would look more attractive backed with evergreens. It is very easy to wire a second real or fake evergreen wreath behind the cone wreath.

It is also possible to insert sprigs of fresh greens 4 or 5 inches long directly into the cone wreath. Cut the stems on a slant and stick them under the outside ring of cones, far enough in so they will not flop over or fall out. You may need to tailor the greens when they are in place to keep the circle even and neat.

# Bow Making

A large bow is an enhancement for almost any wreath, but it must be of suitable size and material. Many textures and colors of ribbon are available. For a 14-inch Pine cone wreath a bow of 3-inch wide velvet ribbon would be handsome. Two-inch ribbon would be better for a 9-inch wreath. Three to five yards will be needed for a large bow.

Have a 15-inch length of wire ready to hold the bow together.

Most ribbon used for wreaths has a right side and a wrong side. The right side of the ribbon should always face you as you work.

Allowing approximately 18 inches for the first streamer, pinch across a single width of ribbon, holding it between the thumb and forefinger of your left hand. The pinched area will become the center of the completed bow.

Form the first loop by raising the ribbon upward, right side facing

you, and allowing it to loop backward until it appears to be the correct size. One loop will be half the width of the completed bow. Again pinch the ribbon at the appropriate spot and crush it together in your left hand with the first pinch.

Twist the ribbon around beneath your thumb so the right side faces front. The ribbon should not need to be turned over again.

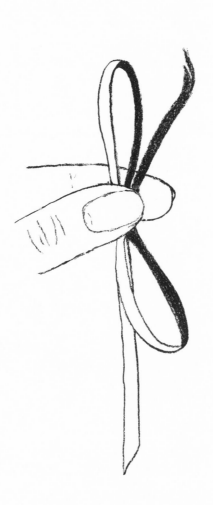

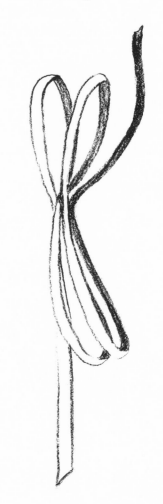

Make a second loop of the same size below your hand. Continue to make alternate loops up and down pushing them sideways into the center of the bow with the fingers of your right hand. The ribbon should loop forward on the top and backward for the bottom loops. There should be either six or eight loops, depending upon how full the bow is to be and how much ribbon you can successfully hold in your hand.

Bring the ribbon over the top of your thumb for one last small loop to hide the gathers. Be sure to catch the ribbon under your thumb and hold it there.

Pass the piece of wire under your thumb and around all the ribbon you are holding, being certain to secure the last small loop. Carry the wire to the back of the bow and twist together as tightly as possible.

Cut one streamer 4 inches shorter than the other. Adjust the bow by spreading the loops.

Both large and small bows can be made this way but wide ribbon is more difficult to hold in your fingers. Practice several times with the same piece of old or inexpensive ribbon before trying a large velvet bow. Some bow makers prefer to make more than one loop in front of the thumb. They make as many as two large loops and one small one. It is a matter of personal preference.

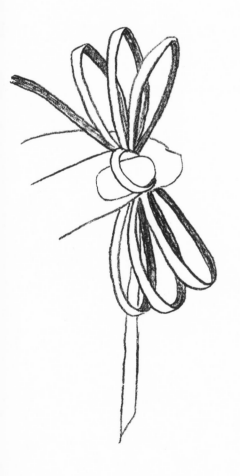

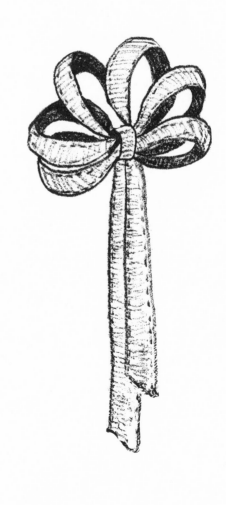

# More Wreaths

*Straw Wreath with Ribbon*

Straw wreaths have become popular in recent years, particularly for use on country style houses. These wreaths are made in Italy and come wrapped in ugly green plastic which should be removed. They are available in several sizes and are so tightly constructed it is difficult to insert even sturdy pole pins into them to hold decorations.

When using a straw wreath be sure to start decorating by attaching a hanger firmly at the top. Next wrap ribbon around the wreath, securing it at intervals with pole pins inserted so they do not show. If Pine cones are to be used, wire them with #24 or heavier wire of sufficient length to be wrapped around the wreath, twisted together in the back and have both ends tucked into the straw.

Many kinds of decorations can be used on these wreaths. Just remember that because straw is not colorful it should be decorated with as many bright ribbons and shiny baubles as possible.

Several years ago I went to a local garden club to talk about Christmas decorations. At that time straw wreaths were very popular so I took along several of different sizes, all still wrapped in their green plastic overcoats. When I began to talk about the straw wreaths I was suddenly aware that the audience had become restless. However, I continued unwrapping the wreaths while explaining that they are made by peasants in Italy. I showed a number of figurines made of corn husks, as well as several sizes and kinds of sliced cones, nuts and pods which could be used to decorate the wreaths. The murmur from the audience was getting louder, so I stopped talking and asked what was wrong. When the explanations died down, I pieced together what had happened.

The year before the club had held a Christmas workshop to make straw wreaths from scratch, and I do mean scratch! They bought some wire and several bales of straw from a feed store and, with no idea how to proceed, attempted to make straw wreaths.

The living room of the house where they met had just been re-decorated. In nothing flat the room was a shambles! Bits and pieces of straw were in every nook and cranny. It soon became obvious that no one was going to leave the house with a finished wreath and the hostess would be spending the next several days cleaning her new furniture. No wonder my exhibit of already-made straw wreaths brought on such moans and groans. These attractive and easy-to-decorate wreaths are surprisingly inexpensive.

The last several years have seen the appearance of wreaths made of Grape vines, Hickory switches, even Honeysuckle and Wisteria. These are very expensive to buy as they must be made by hand, but they can be made at home easily if vines are available.

Look for pieces of vine as long as possible without any major off-shoots, as vines tend to break at those spots. The branches will be easy to handle if they are pre-soaked in a large tub and then stripped of their outer bark. While they are still wet, shape them into rings. Try to weave the vines around each other to give them a little more visual interest. Use raffia or stout cord to bind them together. As long as they are damp they are manageable, so continue to readjust for shape until they are thoroughly dry and stiff. They can always be soaked again and rearranged.

Decorations for these should be rugged in quality and larger than usual to compensate for the sparseness of vines.

You can also wrap a long wet piece of thin de-barked vine tightly around the end of a broomstick. When dry it will look like a coiled spring and can be used, as you would a loop of ribbon, on a wreath or in an arrangement of any kind.

If you prefer you can buy ready-to-decorate wreaths from your florist. These are made of wire in several layers so they have a third dimension. The florist will have stuffed them with Sphagnum moss, bound them with green floral thread and wrapped them with strips of green waxed paper which do not have to be removed. Don't forget to add a hanger if the florist forgot!

It is possible to find the rigid wire frames and stuff them with Sphagnum moss yourself. These wreath frames are excellent to use with fresh evergreens.

Cut the evergreen stems to a point so they can be pushed into the Sphagnum moss more easily. Try to find slim stems so the holes they make will not disturb the shape of the wreath. Each sprig should be 4 to 6 inches long. They will stay fresh much longer if they have been immersed in a container of water for several days before being used.

Greens inserted at random will not be attractive. Make sure they are all going in the same direction.

A large red bow or cluster of Pine cones can be wired to the finished wreath.

# Evergreen Topiary Tree

*Topiary Tree Frame*

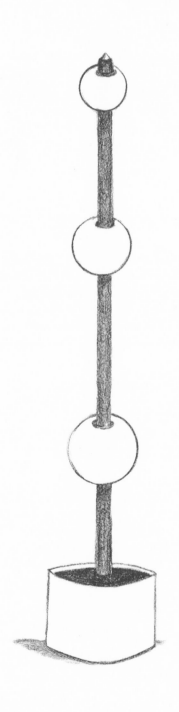

Topiary trees can be very effective standing in tall tubs on either side of a formal entranceway or at the bottom of a flight of stairs. Make these when your evergreens need lots of pruning. They will be more attractive if you do not mix evergreen varieties on the same topiary.

A large redwood tub or a pottery pot 8 to 10 inches tall will be needed. Be sure there is a center hole in the bottom. Take a thick dowel 60 inches long and shave one end to a point. Push the other end into the hole in the pot. Fill the pot with earth and tamp down solidly until the dowel is secure. It might be necessary to put a supporting device on either side of the dowel to keep it erect. Cover your device with earth. Earth is heavy enough to keep the topiary from blowing over in a storm.

Buy three styrofoam balls, 6, 5, and 4 inches in diameter. Force the largest ball down the dowel until it is 8 inches above the rim of the pot. Cut pieces of evergreen 6 inches long, sharpen the stems and push them into the 6-inch ball until the foam is completely obscured.

Force the 5-inch ball down the dowel until it is 6 inches above the greens of the first ball. Completely cover the second ball with 5-inch long pieces of evergreen. Then push the third ball down on the dowel point and add 4-inch greens all over it. When all three balls are finished, trim the greens to make them even.

Decorate the topiary tree with nuts, pods and slices of Pine cones on wires long enough to allow the decorations to rest on the surface of the greens. Or use already-wired silvery glass balls in various colors. If the wires on these balls are wrapped with tape, it will be hard to push them into the styrofoam, so remove this tape before pushing the glass balls in place. Add a green bow of 3-inch wide ribbon to the dowel at the base of the tree. Weather-resistant ribbon is available.

After the Holiday remove the evergreens from the topiary and store it for use another time. Decorated in white or pastel colors, these trees make lovely Summer party decorations.

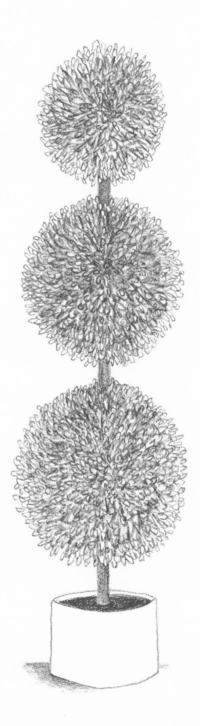

# Door Decorations

*Frame for Spruce Cone Tree*

For double doors a pair of decorations can be used, either just alike or complementary one to the other. At one of our Sales some years ago we made several sets of matching designs suggesting Christmas trees that sold very quickly.

Each tree was made on an 18-inch dowel to which were nailed three very slim V-shaped pieces of Masonite of different sizes. The V's can be pointing either up or down, although they are illustrated with the arms up. The smallest V was 3 inches tall and was nailed 3 inches from the top of the dowel. The middle piece of Masonite was nailed 5 inches below the top piece and the V was 4 inches tall. The bottom and tallest V was 5 inches high and was placed 6 inches below the center V. Four inches of dowel remained at the bottom.

Two large Spruce cones were wired to each V, one on either side with the largest cones at the bottom, medium sized cones in the middle and the smallest ones at the top. The wires were buried in the Spruce cone scales, top and bottom, and twisted together behind the Masonite V's. A piece of Masonite cut to look like a flower pot was nailed to cover the bottom of the dowel. The entire decoration was sprayed gold.

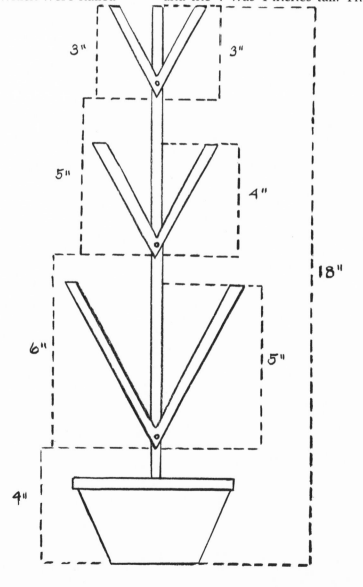

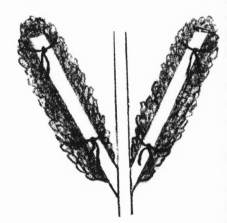

Small 1-inch gold balls were added at the center of each V and the flower pot was trimmed with ribbon.

These trees should be fixed to doors at both top and bottom so they do not swing when the door is opened. This can be done by drilling holes in the top and bottom of each dowel and wiring them to small nails on the door.

Decorating glass doors can be difficult because the reverse side of a wreath or swag is not very attractive and would be seen through the glass from the inside of the house. If you have two wreaths exactly the same size, you can hang one outside and one inside the door, back to back. Then you have decorated the hall, too.

Technically a swag is any decoration for a door which is not round like a wreath. It can be much easier to make than a wreath and generally is a branch of evergreen with an eye-catching object wired on to tickle the imagination of visitors.

Three large Pine cones could be wired together and added to a large bow. I have three huge Coulter Pine cones from California which always attract attention. The large Southern Pine trees which grow from Florida to North Carolina produce cones large enough to be striking when used for the focal point in a swag.

If the owners of the house collect antiques, an ancient salt box or cranberry picker could be filled with greens and attached to the door with a bright bow of ribbon. A set of cart bells is delightful on a swag and it will sing cheery tunes each time the door is opened.

If there are children a fat Santa, an old doll or even a train can be wired to a well-chosen branch.

Pecan nuts wired in bunches to look like Grapes are also delightful wired to a swag. To make them, buy two large bags of Pecans as soon as they appear in the stores in the Fall because that is when lovely pale colored nuts can be found. Both bags may be necessary to supply enough bright brown nuts free from blemishes in the required sizes. Depending upon the size of the nuts and the size of the completed bunch, between 20 and 30 Pecans will be needed.

Before being wired into a bunch, each nut will need to have a hole drilled across its round, or stem, end. Then one end of a 12-inch length of #24 florist wire should be pushed through the hole in each Pecan and twisted around itself close to the nut, leaving a long single wire for a stem. Smear a little white craft glue around the nut near the wired end and wrap brown floral tape around the bottom third of the Pecan and down and around the wire stem.

To form a bunch, lay the stemmed and taped nuts out on a table with the smallest nut with the most pointed end placed so it will become the bottom tip of the bunch. The nuts should graduate upward in size from this nut, having the largest and fattest Pecans at the top of the bunch. When they are all arranged in this manner, gather the stems together in your hand. Adjust the nuts to make the bunch firm and shapely.

Bend the bunched stems over to form a loop for hanging. Twist the wire ends around the group of stems holding the nuts. Squeeze the wire ends as tightly as possible with pliers. Wrap the entire stem, including the loop, with brown floral tape. Spray the nuts several times with clear lacquer before placing it in your design.

During the days when I traveled around the state to speak on Christmas Creations for various garden clubs, I had many amusing and unexpected experiences. Once, when I was winding up one of my speeches, a lady rose and said to me, "Why haven't you got mule muzzles? They are quick and easy to use and very effective."

This took me to many shops selling items created for animals or farmers or both. No one knew where I should go to find one, and many could not imagine why a mule needed a muzzle.

In the course of my travels I did find a pony muzzle. It was made of sturdy metal strands and looked like a basket with a wrongly-placed handle. It turned out to be wonderful to decorate and wire to the door knocker. Greens poked into the wire mesh and a red bow tied to one side of the wire handle made this a quick and easy item. Of course I removed all the buckles and straps.

Then one day I went to visit in Kentucky and suddenly spotted a mule in a muzzle! This muzzle was much larger than a pony muzzle and was made in the shape of a large wire bell. Two of these, wired together at the top and decorated with long red satin streamers, look like a pair of Christmas bells. Pine cones sprayed red or gold, or bright red Christmas balls, can be wired in the openings of the muzzle and a few evergreens added to the ribbon bow, so the door decoration is quickly done. You just have to go where mules are used in agriculture to find a muzzle. These large "bells" are wired to the bridle of the mule because, I am told, mules are indeed ornery creatures and their bite is no joke.

# Inside Decorations

Inside decorations can be made of perishable things like candy canes, candy wrapped in gaily covered foil or angels made of satin and lace.

You might fashion a kissing ball to be hung in the doorway of your living room. Actually it doesn't have to be a ball at all. It could be simply a perky bow with long streamers to which bells are fastened, the bow itself embellished with sprigs of Mistletoe wired or stapled to its center.

Mistletoe is a strange and mysterious plant with berries that are poisonous to human beings. It is a parasite and can destroy the host tree on which it lives by spreading its roots inside the young branches to rob the tree of its nourishment, the sap. The parent plant has a mechanism for shooting the seeds from one host to another. Sometimes birds collect the sticky seeds on their feet and fly to another tree where the seeds are scraped off to begin another infestation.

Lately there has been very little Mistletoe for sale compared to ten or so years ago. Its parasitic nature, its ability to cause the destruction of whole stands of trees and its poisonous properties have made it unwelcome in many parts of the

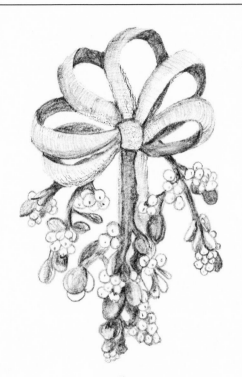

country. It is possible to buy artificial bunches of Mistletoe but so far they do not resemble the real thing and no one is fooled.

The hall table is an ideal place to display a Poinsettia plant and nowadays the flowers come in such lovely colors—crimson, apricot, white, pink and even variegated— that they compliment the decor instead of swearing at it. To use cut Poinsettia flowers in an arrangement, cut them the night before and immerse them, stem up, in water overnight. They will remain fresh for several days in water after this treatment.

A fat candle set into a wreath of cones and pods is attractive on a small table as is a small styrofoam cone covered with acorns or Hemlock cones. Spray the styrofoam brown with special spray that will not disintegrate the foam. Then glue the Acorns or cones to the styrofoam base with white craft glue. Place them as tightly together as possible so the foam does not show. Set the decorated cone in the middle of a fake evergreen wreath. At the end of the Holiday season both can be put into a plastic bag and stored safely for another year.

# Garlands

Artificial evergreen garlands festooned over doorways or cascading down stairways can be wonderfully decorative if they are bountifully enriched with thick groupings of real Pine cones. Because most plastic garlands are so skimpy it would be impossible to wire on too many cones! Fake garlands are made in many varieties—Holly with bright red berries, Boxwood, Spruce, Pine or Cedar. They usually come in 9-foot lengths which can easily be wired together. All kinds of nuts, pods and cones can be used. Just be careful not to twist the wire so tightly that it cuts through the garland. Any extra wire should be removed. Once made, these garlands last for years, but they do take time to make, particularly if an eye-catching focal point is put in the exact center of each garland.

A focal point is a specially built area of interest made of carefully chosen cones and pods wired to the center of the garland. To construct a focal point, cut a piece of hardware cloth about eight inches by four inches and trim off all the sharp edges. You may want to cover the edges with brown floral tape.

Begin the design in the center of the hardware cloth by choosing, perhaps, three Pacfic Coast Sugar Pine cone slices, or three Pinyon Pine cones, and wire them in place. Then wire groups of nuts together and add them to either side of the center cones. You might use Acorns, Pecans, Horse Chestnuts or Peach pits. Next wire long cones such as Norway Spruce or White Pine to both ends, placing them far enough into the hardware cloth so they won't droop. Fill in the remaining area with various sizes of cones and pods. When all is covered, wire the focal point to the center of the garland. If you should ever want to use this focal point in another way, it is easy to attach a wire hanger or loop to the hardware cloth.

To make a charming finishing tassel at each end of a garland, use a grouping of dried Wisteria pods, drilled at the small end, then wired together. If you bring unopened Wisteria pods into your warm house be prepared to experience what sounds like gunfire in the middle of the night when the pods pop, sending their seeds flying in every direction.

The finished garland can be attached to a nail at each top outside end of the hall door molding and then looped up to a nail in the middle of the doorway. Or it could be used on the mantelpiece in the living room. Be sure to support the focal point on an inconspicuous nail in the direct center of the mantel.

I do not have a mantel shelf over the fireplace in my present home so nails must be put in the middle and at both ends of the molding that frames the flush marble facing. For years when my children were small we lived in a huge old turn-of-the-century house where I had eight mantels and mantel shelves to decorate for the Holidays, and I loved doing every one!

My present house is all on one floor so I do not have a lovely curving stairway to decorate. In the big old house, the one with eight mantelpieces, I used several 9-foot garlands wired together to decorate the stairway extending from the first floor to the balcony. These I attached to the handrail with wires twisted together and pushed flat on the underside so there were no loose ends to pierce hands using the rail for support. At the newel post I bunched together real evergreens, adding cones and a huge bow with streamers reaching almost to the floor.

A very handsome garland can be made by wiring a selection of assorted cones and pods onto a base of either heavy 6-ply wire wrapped in brown floral tape or sturdy jute rope just right in texture with Pine cones. A large number of various-sized cones, pods and nuts will be needed to create a garland of sufficient fullness.

Begin this garland by making a loop for hanging at each end of the roping. This can be done by turning the end of the wire or jute back on itself and wrapping it tightly with a dozen or so turns of wire. Cover the area of the binding with tape.

Next decide if your garland is to be made of a random selection of assorted cones and pods or if a design or pattern is to be followed.

If there is to be no design, each cone or pod can be wired as you acquire it, its wire stem wrapped with brown floral tape and the stem, in turn, wrapped around the base roping. All of the wire stems should be of the same length so the finished garland is even and shapely. There should be so many cones that the roping cannot be seen. A garland of this type could grow slowly in length as you bring home pods and seed cases from neighborhood walks or travels through the countryside.

# More Garlands

White Pine Cone Slice      Eastern Hemlock Cone      Sweet Gum Ball

Chestnut Pod      White Pine Cone      Beech Nut Burr

Horse Chestnut      Ponderosa Pine Cone      Persimmon Calyx

A garland planned for a featured location in a doorway, over a mantel or on a sideboard might be designed to be full at each end, tapering toward an interesting focal area in the center. Begin the design for such a garland by creating the focal area in the center, using the largest cones and pods. Then choose two large cones of the same variety, one for each end, and start working from the ends toward the center by choosing ever smaller items—tapering off to the middle, as it were. To keep the design uniform, similar cones or pods should be selected for each side as you move toward the center.

Handsome ribbons wound around at regular intervals greatly enhance a garland's charm. If you use ribbon allow a length of it to stream beyond each end as a finishing touch.

A cone garland can be used in its natural state for a few years, or until it begins to look tired, and then it can be sprayed gold. But remember that gold paint dulls and must be resprayed whenever needed forever after.

Cone garlands are also lovely sprayed with white enamel paint. They will need to be sprayed several times for complete coverage. If you know before you begin making a garland that it is to be painted, each cone or pod can be dipped into enamel paint and allowed to dry before being wired. A cone may need to be dipped several times before all the surfaces are covered. Use floral tape of matching color to cover the wires.

A charming garland can be created using real fruit among the cones. Around Thanksgiving time I search for Pomegranates with their attractive crowns still intact.

These will last a long time, slowly drying and becoming hard, so it is necessary to push a wire through them while they are still fresh and tender. I wire them into garlands so their tops are visible. After the Holidays I put them away for another year. If they lose their lovely red color, I polish them with lipstick to extend their attractiveness for several years.

Red Apples, rubbed so they shine, are also effective wired into a garland, but they will slowly disintegrate and must be removed after a week or so. This also applies to hard green Pears. Onions and Potatoes are fairly long-lasting.

Dried Artichokes offer another interesting shape. They can be sprayed gold, as can Lotus pods. Chestnut burrs, though hard to handle because of their spines, add a different texture as do Horse Chestnuts, either in their husks or without them.

I use White Pine cones cut into slices which look rather like open-faced flowers to make another kind of garland. As it takes more than one hundred cones to produce one of these garlands, I make them only in years when the White Pine trees have been particularly productive.

First the cones must be brushed to remove all dirt. Then they are placed in a preheated 200° oven on a piece of aluminum foil for 20 minutes to melt the sticky white resin which covers White Pine cones. As the resin melts it becomes a clear glaze on the tips of the scales. If you attempt to wash the dirt from cones the scales will close and it will be several days before they dry and open up again.

With a pair of sturdy wire nippers, cut each White Pine cone into as many slices as the length of the cone will allow, usually three to five slices per cone. Each slice should have at least two full rows

of scales. Because the wires on this kind of garland may be visible, wrap each 6-inch length of #24 wire with brown floral tape before attaching it to the cone slice. Run the wrapped wire around the bottom row of scales, pulling it around the center core and twisting it tightly to make a stem.

With the cone slices prepared, I am ready to begin making the garland. Cutting 7 feet of 6-ply wire, I first bind each end of the wire into a loop for hanging before wrapping the entire length in brown floral tape. Then it is just a matter of placing each wired pine cone slice against the 6-ply wire roping, twisting the stem around the core several times, round and round, row after row, until the entire garland is completed.

I use these garlands in their natural state, but they could be gussied up with velvet bows or shiny red balls an inch or so in diameter.

Slices of White Pine cones also make attractive "flower" arrangements if they are painted with enamel paint in flower colors and their wire stems wrapped with floral tape. Velvet leaves may be added for glamour. A basket of them makes a lovely gift and looks charming wherever placed.

# Christmas

The year we moved into our present house our Christmas tree, drier than we realized, caught fire because of electrical difficulties and we only narrowly escaped disaster. Ever since then we have bought only living Christmas trees and have successfully transplanted all but two of them in eighteen years. Now we look with pride at the handsome one-of-a-kind evergreens, some already more than twenty feet tall, which encircle our acre of ground.

Sadly, though, all the lovely old decorations we had, some from my babyhood, were destroyed by the fire, including the darling wax angel we used to put on the top of the tree. At the time of the fire we had a delightful and beloved Siamese cat named Anna, as in *Anna and the King of Siam.* Anna much enjoyed batting Christmas balls off the tree, so after the fire we began replacing our lovely fragile glass ornaments with unbreakable balls and garlands.

Kind friends contributed balls with our children's names on them, Japanese fans and other Oriental knickknacks, as well as hand made ornaments of their own design, making our tree a treasured mishmash of loving memories.

By necessity I became aware of things long packed away in an old attic trunk: my mother's little white baby slippers, highbutton shoes worn by an uncle in the 1870's, small leather gloves only three inches long, a well-worn dog collar from a long-gone family friend, and many other mementos of our past. What fun it has been to bring these out each year and hang them on the tree!

Making cookie hands has also become a tradition with us. These are made by having each child in the family place his or her hand on extra-stiff cookie dough, rolled out to a thickness of 1/4 inch, while a pattern is traced around the fingers and wrist with a small knife. Each cookie hand needs a hole punched at the wrist before baking so it can be tied with a ribbon to the tree.

Because of our fire no lights have ever again been placed on the tree. Instead, three floodlights are played into the area, one in the middle at the ceiling level and two on either side at the floor. These pick up the glitter of silver garlands, shiny chains and brilliant balls. We also make a point of decorating the side of the tree next to the bay window so our neighbors may enjoy its beauty with us.

Last Christmas we bought a new artificial garland for our living room. Made of the same material with which silk flowers are made, it is a lovely muted green color, large and fluffy, and is charming over Great Grandmother's black and gold mirror. To decorate it, we wired on some small brass stars, gold-colored cupids and small shiny gold metal baskets. It never sagged or lost a needle, and is happily put away in its own box to be used, hopefully, for many years to come.

If you have open book shelves, either in your living room or den, they are a perfect place to display your Christmas cards. Cards are too attractive to be piled in a basket, one on top of another. They do a beautiful job of decorating a whole room if they are put where they can be seen.

The biggest and most beautiful cones can be put on these shelves, too, to make a break in a long line of cards. It would be interesting to identify the cones with small slips of paper tucked in the scales.

A very attractive small decoration can be created by mounting a single large Loblolly or Bull Pine cone on a dowel inserted in a small block of wood. The cone is then decorated by having tiny fake fruit, Christmas balls, nuts, cones or bits of glitter glued onto its scales.

Drill a hole in the center of the bottom of the Pine cone and another hole of the same size in the center of the wooden base. A 2 or 3-inch length of dowel is glued into these holes to make the trunk of the little Pine cone "tree." My husband makes the bases of these trees for me from small pieces of scrap wood. Similar bases might be obtained reasonably from a lumber yard where they frequently discard such bits of wood as scrap.

Let the glue dry for at least an hour before the decorating begins. The trees can be left natural or they can be sprayed with clear lacquer, gold or white enamel paint. They can be trimmed with all-of-one-kind decorations such as green velvet bows, silver balls or tiny red birds, or they can have a colorful mixture of miniature ornaments. Glue a piece of ribbon around the base and tie a bow around the dowel. A small cluster of balls or cones could be added to the bow. Decorating these little trees is so much fun you will want to do more than one.

Several years ago my sister trimmed a pretty shallow straw basket as a gift for me. She has always saved the handsome Christmas cards she receives and for this decoration she used the reproduction of a Renaissance painting of Mother and Child bordered in gold from one of the cards.

First she stained the natural straw a light mahoghany color and painted the rim gold. She wired a hanger onto the back of the basket, trimmed the card to fit inside the bottom and carefully pasted the picture in place with white craft glue.

Around the picture she glued a frame of tiny nuts, pods and cones, the largest no bigger than a Hemlock cone. At the base of the picture she glued a collection of larger cones and pods to make a focal point. My basket has become a treasured keepsake.

One of the truly unique little Christmas trees we make for our Sale is constructed of small branches, 12 to 14 inches in length, cut from the Trifoliate Orange, *Poncirus trifoliate,* a very thorny shrub which is hardy as far north as Maryland. All present-day Orange trees were first successfully grown on the root stock of this plant.

Because of its long stiff thorns Trifoliate Orange plants would make an impenetrable hedge, more daunting than the one which protected Sleeping Beauty. I find it very painful to deal with but, armed with padded gloves, I have pruned my one plant for use at our Sales year after year.

For the base of this decoration use a small flower pot, the hole in the bottom sealed with a piece of foil. Hold the thorny branch firmly in the center of the pot and pour plaster of Paris, mixed according to the directions on the package, around the branch. It is best to hold onto the branch rather than the pot as the plaster becomes red hot when it is mixed with water. Let the plaster dry overnight before testing to see if it is hard and the tree ready to decorate.

Spray the tree and pot bright gold. Then assemble the decorations: artificial fruit—preferably small gold and green pears; small feathered birds; tiny green satin leaves that come in bunches in a craft store; and, if you can find them at a florist supply house, sprays of delicately beaded wires called pearl swirls. If pearl swirls are not available, use small glass balls.

First the pears are wired onto the branches, followed by the small green leaves. Fill in the remaining bare spaces with the delightfully airy pearl swirls. One bird—a partridge or something similar—might be placed at the bottom sitting on the plaster, another perched on a branch. Sheet moss can be placed around the base of the branch.

Attractive branches from other kinds of trees could be used, although we have found the Trifoliate Orange very satisfactory, and other colors of spray paint may better suit your decor. Your tree could be completely decorated with small birds, Christmas tree balls, glass bells, candy gum drops, red velvet bows, or all of them together. Experiment! This decoration and all the others in this book should be planned to suit your interest and your home.

For those who have a fireplace, a decorative firescreen is delightful to own. Because the decorations are flammable, however, this is a screen to be used when a fire is not burning.

Measure the size of your fireplace opening. Then buy a length of hardware cloth to fit the opening and cut it into the shape of an arch. Buy two or three angle irons of the largest size you can find and fasten them to the bottom edge of the screen with wire. The third one will be needed for the middle if the fireplace is wide, as larger screens have a tendency to buckle unless supported.

Spray the hardware cloth and feet black. You may prefer gold, but gold will darken and need to be resprayed within a year.

A border of cones wired around the periphery of the screen will help to cover the ragged edges and also serve as a frame. Long cones, such as Norway Spruce, should be wired at each end and placed so they lie lengthwise along the edge, all going in the same direction. Short, flat-bottomed cones should be placed around the edge of the screen with their tips facing front and their bottom row of scales hooked over the edge. Only one wire will be needed to hold each of these cones in place. If the edge of the hardware cloth is going to show, it should be covered with brown floral tape.

Only the center of a firescreen need be decorated. An assortment of large cone slices and whole cones, some turned to show their attractive base whorls together with a few unusual pods and some small nuts and cones bunched together will give a most attractive effect. It is possible to add dried Magnolia leaves, Corn husks or dried grasses to extend the design. If the center design is not large enough to fill the screen, add small groupings of cones in each of the four corners.

To add yet another Holiday note, fill a pretty basket with leftover, even damaged, Pine cones. Tie or wire a bright red ribbon to the handle and put it near the hearth to be used to encourage reluctant fires.

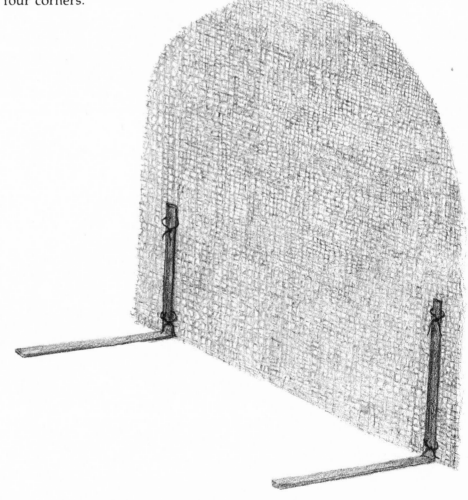

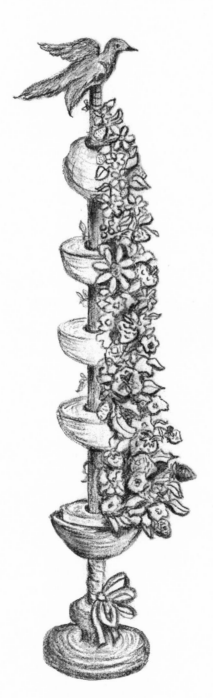

Last summer I visited an attractive seashore Christmas shop where there were many charming imported decorations from Germany for sale. Among them were beautiful red plastic Strawberries with loops of gold cord for hangers. I was told the following story about them.

In pre-war Germany, among the wealthy and titled of the land, it was the fashion to have gardeners set out Strawberry plants in greenhouses in order to provide berries of enormous size to be hung on the Christmas tree. The idea was so popular that children whose parents could not afford a greenhouse and gardener began to feel deprived. So the German makers of Christmas tree balls began to make charming glass Strawberries, not so expensive, and usable year after year. I had one as a child. It had shiny white seeds that glittered like snow all over it. The unbreakable plastic berries I bought at the Christmas shop came in assorted sizes and I designed a topiary tree last fall using strawberries of three sizes.

A 24-inch long dowel with a 3/4-inch diameter was sharpened to a point on one end. The blunt end was then glued into a hole drilled in a wooden vase-shaped base which was painted a dull blue-green with gold edges. A 7-inch gold-colored metal florist bowl was punctured in the exact center and pushed down the dowel.

Next, two styrofoam balls, one 4-inch and one 3-inch, were sliced in half and pushed down the dowel, cut side up, the two large halves first, each of them 3 inches apart. A final uncut 2-inch styrofoam ball was pushed over the dowel, with the point showing several inches above the top.

The styrofoam balls were then completely studded with small green velvet leaves on short wires, available at a craft store. Strawberries and clusters of very small Grapes were added and, finally, assorted small white Strawberry flowers. Everything was held in place with pole pins. The final effect was a charming spiral hodgepodge of fruit and flowers.

At the very top I added a 6-inch white dove. The exposed dowel was wrapped in a piece of red velvet ribbon and the tip smeared with glue. The breast of the bird was pushed onto the point.

This gay decoration can be used on the table, a chest, or anywhere in the house. The addition of fruit and flowers keeps it from looking too seasonal, so it can be used year-round.

One year it was my job to buy the findings for one of our Christmas Sales, and I came upon a group of 7-inch tall Bambi-type deer, Walt Disney variety, which had been greatly reduced in price. They could not be returned, but I bought them anyway and then worried for fear I had wasted the club's money. The Bambis were covered in some sort of synthetic material which looked only vaguely like a deer's coat. It was not very attractive, so I thought if I covered them with something more natural they would be easier to sell. Pine cone petals or, more properly, scales, came to mind and there were many cones in my cellar with which to practice. I found Norway Spruce cones to be the best. Each cone has a variety of scale sizes, all of which are thin enough to conform to curved surfaces. Next I experimented with glues and pastes and ultimately found that white craft glue works well and leaves no residue.

Scales from three large Spruce cones are enough to cover a 7-inch deer. To remove scales from the cones, use a sharp instrument which will fit under the scales without breaking them. I have a wonderful pair of Japanese flower scissors which are perfect for the job, but they are hard to find and expensive. The best substitute seems to be small wire nippers which are generally available at any hardware store.

Start from the stem end of the cone and carefully flick off each scale. The tip ends are useful in covering the legs, but leave them on the cone so they are not lost before you are ready to use them. If your cones do not produce enough small scales for the legs, carefully cut the larger scales to fit. The legs are somewhat difficult so I am apt to do them last, after the body and head are covered.

Start applying the scales at the middle of the deer's back and work down the sides, applying scales as if they were shingles, row after row, leaving the stomach area until last.

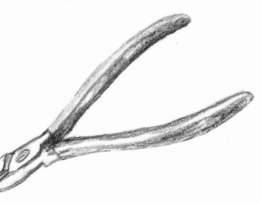

This can be very time-consuming, but I have discovered some shortcuts. For instance, I work on two or three animals at one time, because after several rows of scales have been glued, they begin to slip and slide. When this happens I put that deer aside and work on another one.

When the back and sides are covered, start to work on the head. Leaving the front tip of the deer's nose uncovered, work toward the cheeks. Do not cover the eyes. Work up to the ears, using one good-sized scale to cover the interior of the ear. Also fit one scale in the area between the ears. Cut it to fit, if necessary.

At the base of the neck begin gluing scales, point down, on the collar line and work up to the top of the head, overlapping back and sides. Cover the back of each ear with one large scale.

After doing the head, I generally glue a row of scales down the middle of the back to cover the area where the sides come together. Start this just at the tail and work toward the head.

Next I tackle the stomach area and the legs. The former is just a matter of covering the material of which the deer is made.

Because the legs are so slender, the scales chosen to cover them often have to be cut to fit. Start at the feet and overlap like the body scales until all is covered.

In the case of the Bambi deer, I found that the ears were not large enough to be seen when the scales were applied, so I glued on two small Hemlock cones to accent the area. This gives the deer a perky look.

Be sure to buy deer which stand on four feet. There are some for sale with a lifted foot, but these need to be fastened to a base in order to stand alone.

In the north wall of my living room there is a fairly large window where I hang my favorite nut and cone wreath, backed with evergreens from my own property. In the open center I fasten a scale-covered stag. I always think it looks as if the deer is just coming out of the forest, maybe looking for Dancer, Prancer, and the rest!

Birds, ducks and geese in various sizes suitable to be used on wreaths and swags can also be covered with scales. Often these are partly covered with real feathers, especially the wings and tails. In the year of the Bicentennial I found a wonderful eagle. It is very attractive but I have never found another.

Leaving the bird's throat uncovered, I start at the top of the head, gluing the scales down to the neck before beginning to encircle the entire body. The scales are put on with the ends pointed toward the tail. I usually cover most of the underside, the back and the tops of the wings. Do not try to glue scales over the feathers.

Large plastic or molded paperboard ducks can be covered with scales, as can squirrels, rabbits or bears. Animal figures such as these are sometimes available as fuzzy-covered banks. I think only woodsy looking animals look well covered in this way.

It is important to follow the line of the animal's form with the direction of the scales. In the case of a large duck, the scales should lie in the direction that feathers would normally lie, and a change in variety of scales, from Norway Spruce scales to White Pine scales for instance, could differentiate between wing feathers and breast feathers. If possible I draw guidelines on the object I am covering, then place a row of scales along the line, filling in behind the first row with similar ones.

# The Dining Room

A special room in any house at Holiday time is the dining room. Here you can go all out, perhaps using a tablecloth you have made yourself. Our garden club has produced some fabulous ones for exhibition tables. The most spectacular, bought in New York City, was made of white felt embroidered around the border with gold thread in a design depicting lighted Christmas trees and wreaths. Small flame-shaped bulbs were pushed through tiny holes in the trees and wreaths from the underside, all part of a string of lights which, when plugged in, twinkled merrily. The cloth was oval in shape and I have always wanted to duplicate it, my greatest problem being the size required to fit a table accomodating a family of fourteen plus a friend or two.

The decoration used in the center of the table with the white felt cloth was a slim 18-inch gold tree. To make this a styrofoam cone was sprayed gold and ornamented with green velvet leaves and small gold balls, both of which had short wire stems inserted at random into the golden cone.

One year my sister and I planned a table decoration featuring peppermint candy canes hanging from the upper and lower rims of an epergne. We constructed the epergne by standing a tall slim glass vase in a short glass compote, holding it in place with floral clay. Several dozen 4-inch candy canes were hung around the rim of the top container so tightly together

that the edge was completely covered. Twice as many 5-inch canes were needed to encircle the edge of the lower container in a similar manner. The top vase held an arrangement of small red and white Carnations and the lower container was filled with regular-sized ones. Both containers held water for the flowers.

For this table we made a cloth of red and white striped cotton edged with red ball fringe, and the four candlesticks on the table continued the theme by holding different colored candles—two red and two white. The cloth was later used many times by my teenagers for supper parties. It washed beautifully so there were no heartaches over spills.

Another year, a spectacular cloth of white satin was made by the same members who found the twinkling cloth. First the edge was trimmed with gold fringe and with this white and gold china was used for the place settings. The second time the cloth appeared, it was bordered with red velvet ribbon and the centerpiece was a beautiful white china Madonna decorated with handsome American Beauty Roses. Plain white china looked well here.

Perhaps the most successful Christmas table these ladies ever exhibited had a 2-foot live evergreen tree as its centerpiece. The only decoration on the tree was a restrained dusting of fake snow. Three charming 8-inch deer covered with Pine cone scales

reclined at the base of the tree on a tablecloth of forest green. The deer were bought in Switzerland and were the inspiration for the much smaller ones mentioned earlier.

On either side of the tree a slender 12-inch S-curve of cones and nuts was placed, each holding three red candles. The S-curves were cut from 1/4 inch thick Masonite which was drilled over its entire surface with holes. The decorations were wired into place just as they would be on a Masonite wreath ring. Two candles were at one end of the S-curve and one at the other. A place was created to hold the candles by wiring the cones and pods tightly around used candle stubs which were replaced with new candles when the decoration was complete.

The wires for this decoration must be pressed close to the base on the back and, when all is covered on the top, the underside should be backed with felt. It is easy to cut the felt to fit if it is measured before the base is decorated.

One year, at the last possible moment, I was asked to do a table for a New Year's Eve party—something quick and easy! After feverish trials and errors, I devised the following. I found an oval antique gold picture frame, about 15 inches long, and placed it in the center of a bright green organdy tablecloth. In the middle of the cloth, several inches outside the rim of the frame, I sewed an outline of gold sequins which came on a long gold ribbon.

Two Pineapples were laid end-to-end inside the oval picture frame so their leafy tops curled over either end. Then two beautiful full bunches of red Grapes were placed over the area where the two Pineapples met. These were crowned with two smaller bunches of green Grapes and my decoration was complete. To add more excitement to the picture, take several bunches of small Christmas balls on wires—the kind florists use to insert in their Holiday arrangements—and push them into the Pineapple eyes. Remove foil from the wires before you try to stick them into the fruit.

Around my centerpiece I used four tall glass candle holders sprayed with gold paint, the pale green candles decorated at the base with wired-on bunches of small green Grapes and tiny gold balls. This would do for any festive Holiday table.

My grandmother set a delightfully simple table for Christmas dinner. Her cloth was of Irish damask, the napkins matching and 36 inches square! Down the length of the table and across the middle of it she placed 4-inch wide red satin ribbons, which made it look like a huge Christmas package. As she was married in the 1860's all of her silver was Victorian and ornate so the simplicity of her Holiday decorations was dramatic. The center arrangement was made of

red Carnations in an elaborate silver epergne. (In my opinion it is impossible to make an unattractive decoration using an epergne.) With the addition of pretty party favors at each place, the entire display took very little time to achieve.

Christmas was always a gala event in my life, and for my siblings, too, because our mother loved it. Our lovely home was decorated top to bottom, and presents for the whole family made a sizable pile. One would think that was more than enough, but no indeed! After all the packages were opened and a delicious dinner eaten, everyone waited impatiently for Mother to strip the small Christmas tree which graced the center of the table. Around the base of this tree were piled small packages, prettily beribboned and marked with the names of all present. The contents had been chosen with great imagination and were either useful or fun. It was our mother's joy in the Holiday season and her interesting and unusual decorations that inspired both my sister and me to emulate her in our own family celebrations and home decorations.

Here are a few suggestions for setting an attractive table.

1. A tablecloth may have one crease down the middle. All others should be ironed out.

2. The cloth for a dining table should hang 12 to 18 inches below the table edge.

3. Placemats should not overlap. Twenty-four inches from the center of one mat to the center of the next mat is the ideal spacing.

4. If napkins are folded like a book, the open edges should face the plate.

5. Candles are never used on a luncheon table. They may be used on a tea table, but only if needed. For a seated meal the flame should never be at eye level.

6. The decorative unit or centerpiece should not be longer than one-third of the table length. The arrangement may be different on each side, but it must be finished all the way around.

7. The height of the centerpiece of a dining table should not be taller than 18 inches, which is roughly the distance from elbow to fingertips.

8. Buffet table decorations are unlimited in height and may be placed on the table wherever they look best. They are usually taller and more imposing than designs for a seated meal because they are seen by people who are standing. They must be completed on both sides.

9. The cloth for a buffet table may be longer than normal, but should never touch the floor.

10. In a tablecloth beware of bold patterns which may detract from decorations. If lace is used, choose an undercloth of matching color. Even damask designs can inject unexpected confusion.

A decoration I used many times on our Christmas table was an Apple tree. We were lucky enough, when we lived in the big old house, to have several wonderful varieties of very old Apple trees. Our favorite was called Black Twig and the fruit of this tree we prized for its long-keeping properties.

In those days it was easy to buy, for 50 cents, a quarter-bushel basket. This I placed upside down on a lazy Susan. The Apples, at least three dozen of them, were rubbed with a piece of flannel until they shone and then divided into three piles—large, medium and small.

Around the bottom of the upside-down basket I arranged a row of the largest apples, testing them for fit. When they were in position cocktail picks, fat in the middle and pointed at each end, were inserted between the Apples to hold them in place. For the second row the same procedure was followed, using slightly smaller Apples. Every second or third Apple I added a pick from the second row to the first to steady the upper row. This continued until the peak of the basket was reached.

Sometimes I picked together a pyramid of the smallest Apples for the top of the basket. Occasionally I bought a handsome Pineapple and stood it straight up, inserting picks from the base of the Pineapple into the Apples below to strengthen the construction.

When the Apple tree was finished I placed a circle of Holly around the base and added small sprigs of Holly between the Apples where they were needed to hide the quarter-bushel basket. This decoration, made of long-lasting Apples, will be attractive from Thanksgiving through New Year's Day before going to pieces.

# A Crescent Decoration

Okra Pods
Horse Chestnuts
Mango Seed

Gourd
Coconut
Acorns
English Walnuts
Dried Pineapple
Fungus
Peach Pits

58

Magnolia Pod
Black Walnut Husk
Teasel
Lotus Pod
Jacaranda Pod
Avocado Seed
Artichoke

Many Varieties of Cones
Other Unusual Items

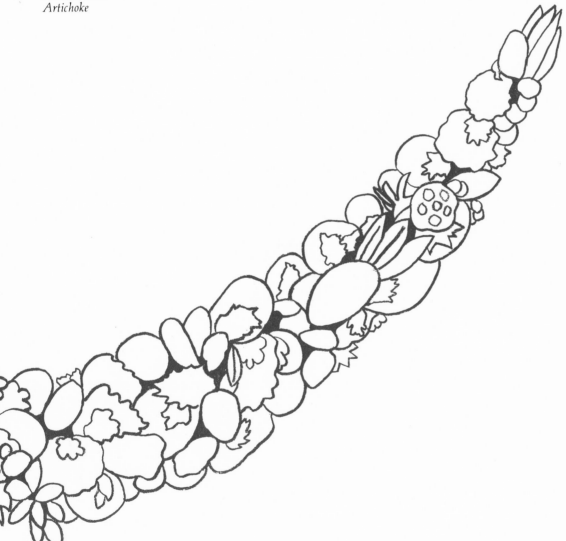

*Pin Oak Acorn*

*Scarlet Oak Acorn*

*Peach Pit*

Most dining rooms have a sideboard or chest of some kind which is a very attractive place to decorate. There is a raised shelf at each end of my sideboard which gives me a place to use a pair of matching decorations.

Over the center of the sideboard I hang a special ornament more than 25 years old. It was made from a piece of 1/4-inch plywood cut in the shape of a 5-foot long crescent drilled all over with holes 1 inch apart.

At each pointed end of the crescent I wired a cluster of 6-inch Okra pods. These had been allowed to remain on the plants until too woody to be edible so they were tough enough not to disintegrate.

Several times I have suggested wiring together nuts of several kinds so they resemble bunches of Grapes. Any kind of Acorn can be used for this, as well as Peach pits and Horse Chestnuts. These add a different and interesting accent wherever you use them. Some nuts, such as Almonds in their shells, do not last well because the shells become tattered on the edges. In the central focal area of the crescent, I used bunches of Horse Chestnuts. I also used a collection of immature Coconuts, from 2 to 6 inches in length, found on a Florida beach.

With such a large area to cover, it was helpful to find and wire in unusual items—dried Pineapples, for instance. They added a large oblong shape to contrast with the many round Pine cones that were used.

To dry Pineapples, find small-sized ones, not miniature, but not the largest, either. They should not be overly ripe. Put them in a sunny dry window. A South-facing conservatory, or just a regular

room, will do. Put each Pineapple in a shallow bowl with sides no more than 2 inches high. Every week turn a different side of the fruit toward the sun and continue to do this for quite a few weeks.

In the midst of my first effort to dry a Pineapple, my husband suddenly announced that he expected to be bitten by a Tse-tse fly following which he would die of sleeping sickness! He led me to the little conservatory and I found it filled with irritating, but not deadly, flying fruit flies. They were helping to rid the fruit of its juices, thereby speeding the drying process.

It takes more than a month to produce a hard, sturdy, long-lasting dried Pineapple, and it is a good idea to insert a wire across the base of the fruit before it is too dry and hard. If the wire is difficult to twist together once it is put through the Pineapple, use a pair of pliers.

I used several Lotus pods in my crescent which were purchased from a florist shop. These are not as durable as Pine cones, so they needed to be tucked up against some larger object for protection. I drilled mine across the narrow end of the stem, wired them and backed them up against the Pineapples so they would not get frayed edges from sticking out above everything around them.

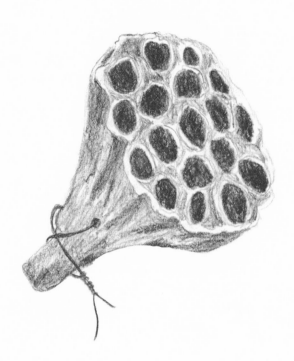

One Christmas one of my husband's clients sent us some huge English Walnuts at least 3 inches in diameter. We opened them carefully, enjoyed their delicious meats, and then glued the shells back together again. They still remind us of a long-ago kindness and, wired into the crescent, are particularly attractive.

Another decorative item I used was an Artichoke. This vegetable can be dried and used just as you buy it or, by carefully using your fingers to pull open the leaves, the center choke can be exposed. To keep the leaves from closing again stuff facial tissue between them until they are dry.

Put the Artichoke on a board in a warm place to dry. Before it is completely dry, insert a wire across the stem end so you can attach it to whatever base you choose. (It could even be wired to the top of a long stick for use in dried flower arrangements.) I used an opened Artichoke in the focal area of my crescent and an unopened one at each end.

One of my favorite nuts is the Acorn from the Burr Oak which looks like it is wearing a fringed hat. Because the cup is likely to come off, I separate the nut from its cup in advance, drill across the cup for wiring, insert the wire, twist it firmly on the outside of the cap and then glue the nut back into its cup. I am lucky to have a friend with a Burr Oak tree who calls me in the Fall when the nuts begin to come rattling down. The squirrels and I have a contest to see who can collect the most.

Jacarandas are among my favorite pods. They can be used closed or carefully pried open so that there are two beautifully patterned halves to work with. Either whole or half, they can be drilled 1/2 inch from the stem end and wired for use. Together with the large flat seeds from Mango fruit, which dry attractively, they are useful to fill long narrow bare spots left between cones. Or try drying an Avocado seed—it can provide a lovely peach-colored ball.

Sometimes the stem end of a Pine cone is interesting and using it turned upside down adds variety to a decoration. When you slice any kind of cone look at both ends. You may be glad you did.

To cover a large area such as the crescent a great assortment of material was needed. Added to Pine cones of many varieties, I used such things as pieces of dried fungus, Jimpson weed pods, Teasels, Sterculia pods, Black Walnuts in their husks, and several Gourds. Tiny Larch and Hemlock cones were handy to fill in holes. They were put in place with white craft glue.

When my crescent was several years old I sprayed it gold. But a word of caution. Never, never use any aerosol spray indoors. It can be lethal!

# The Kitchen

*Wooden Spoon*
*ready for spicy decorations*

By the time I am ready to consider decorations for the kitchen my enthusiasm is somewhat diminished, but the door is a must because everyone uses it rather than the front door.

Recently the back door has been dedicated to the loving and beloved pets in our lives. A small 10-inch straw wreath is wrapped with 2-inch plaid ribbon in the Stewart pattern which my husband proudly claims. Tucked into the ribbon at intervals are doggy bones, easily removed on demand. A catnip mouse is wired onto the bow for you-know-whom.

For the kitchen window fresh homegrown evergreens, excepting always Hemlock which loses its needles so soon, are wired onto a florist's wire wreath which is then decorated with kitchen items such as cookie cutters, knife, fork and spoon, and a bright red plastic bow. The humidity in the area over the sink keeps the greens fresh, but would disintegrate Pine cones or other dried material and turn a satin bow into a dishrag.

To hang a window wreath, I hammer a thin 2 1/2-inch nail into the window frame. In a double-hung window it can stand up in front of the lock. I keep my nail in place the year round.

My kitchen is on the small side, but I do have a wall where I hang one decoration. The base for this is a 14-inch wooden spoon with a hole drilled through the end of the handle and four holes drilled in the bowl of the spoon.

A decorative bow is wired through the hole in the handle with a hanger hidden behind the bow.

Half of a 2-inch styrofoam ball is wired onto the spoon, using the holes drilled there. Around the edge of the styrofoam a fringe of German Statice is poked. I use the small-flowered variety in off-white. A few additional pieces of Statice can be added to the middle of the foam.

Pieces of Ginger in interesting shapes are wrapped with wire and their wire stems pushed into the foam. Three-inch rolls of Cinnamon bark can be wired and inserted, as well as clusters of Bayleaves and wired Cardamon seeds. Cloves, singly or in groups, can be pushed in where they are needed to hide the styrofoam. Let your imagination run riot with your own spice spoon!

Another wall decoration can be fashioned by cutting a piece of 1/2-inch mesh hardware cloth into the shape of a tall slim Christmas tree. Heavy shears or wire cutters will be needed to cut the hardware cloth. The size of the tree should be determined by the size of the area you are decorating.

Cut a dowel long enough to reach from the top of the tree to 6 inches below the bottom edge. One inch from the top of the dowel a hole should be drilled. Fix the dowel down the center of the hardware cloth tree by lacing a wire around the dowel and through the mesh, securing the wire first at the hole. Use the small hole to make a hanger.

Next, Magnolia leaves are sewed over the surface of the hardware cloth. Dyed dark green and permanently supple, dried Magnolia leaves can be bought by the piece or by the box at the florist. Using a sharp-point, large-eye needle

threaded with heavy green florist thread, sew the leaves flat against the hardware cloth in rows. Begin at the top with a single leaf pointed up. Fan the leaves out from that point until they are resting horizontally along the base of the tree. Be sure to cover all raw edges of the hardware cloth with the Magnolia leaves.

An interesting selection of cones, nuts and pods should be wired to the center of the tree in a tall thin pyramid with the larger items at the bottom and in the center.

A group of Pecans wired like a cluster of Grapes is attractive in the center of the bottom edge. A cluster of cone slices in a variety of sizes can be wired above the Pecans.

The cones should be wired through the hardware cloth and the Magnolia leaves. Be sure to use long thin cones at the outside edges of the design. This handsome and elegant decoration could also be used on a door.

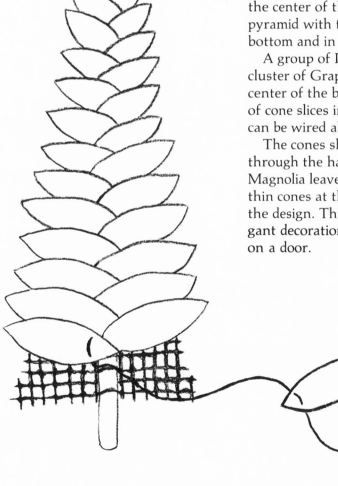

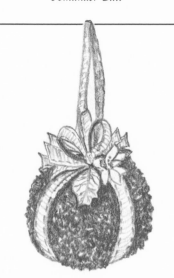

Years ago our garden club discovered that pomander balls were a very popular item at the Christmas Sale. These are made with an Orange as a base. Do not use Navel Oranges which can be pithy. Lemons are not satisfactory either. They contain a goodly amount of juice and, if poked full of holes, the peel shrinks and loses its shape as the Lemon juice leaks out.

Pomander balls take a great many Cloves, so try to find a supplier that packages them in pound-size containers.

With a thin sturdy punch such as a nut pick, make holes in the Orange so close together that when the Cloves are inserted no space on the Orange can be seen. Once the ball is completely covered with Cloves, tie a ribbon both ways around the Orange and add a pretty bow on top. Attractive small fake flowers can be tucked into the bow. If the pomander ball is to be hung, a wire can be run around the ball under the ribbon so it will not show. If desired, ground spices mixed with Orris root can be patted over the Cloves before the ribbon is added. These balls are thought to repel moths so they can not only be attractive, but useful as well. They make lovely gifts.

Fascinating "flowers" with Pine cone centers and dried Sweet Potato slices for petals are fun to make and use. Choose long slim Sweet Potatoes to make the petals. Look for ones that are about 2 inches in diameter and cut them into slices between 1/4 and 1/8 of an inch thick. Place the Potato slices on a cookie sheet and put them in a 200° oven until the slices feel dry but are not brown; or put the cookie sheet in the hot sun, turning the slices from time to time until they are completely dry.

Short, squat Pine cones, such as Black, Red or Mugo cones, will be needed for the centers. They should be about 2 inches in diameter and 2 inches tall.

Cut a wire 24 inches long for each "flower." Fold the wire in half and place the fold around the base of a cone, pulling the wire tight against the core of the cone and twisting it together to form a long stem. The stem will come from the side of the cone and the top of the cone will face sideways like a daffodil. Wrap the wire stem with brown floral tape.

Next choose the dried Sweet Potato slices to form the petals around the Pine cone center. It will take about five slices. They should overlap slightly when inserted between the Pine cone scales. After they have been tentatively placed in position around the cone, remove each Potato slice and smear it with a little white craft glue to fix it permanently in position.

These flowers are attractive in dried flower arrangements or, with shortened stems, they can be used to decorate a wreath or swag.

# A Pine Cone Tree

*Designed By Mrs. Daniel Murray Cheston III*

**Materials:**
Hardware cloth, 1/2 inch mesh
#24 Florist Wire
Sphagnum moss
Two-inch wooden florist picks with wires attached. Four-inch picks can be used if they are broken in half.
White craft glue
Twelve-inch square of heavy cardboard
Dozens of small, flat-bottomed Pine cones of the same variety in different sizes.

This Pine cone tree will look fresh and Christmassy for a long time. It can be used as a centerpiece for the dining room table, on a piano, on a small table, anywhere. I have made a toy-filled tree for each of my grandchildren and I expect them to last, if properly cared for, for their children.

The base for this design is a 15-inch cone of hardware cloth. To make a cone, first draw a newspaper pattern for a quarter-circle with a 15-inch radius. Lay the pattern along the edges of a piece of hardware cloth and cut around it with wire cutters. Push the two straight edges of the quarter-circle toward each other and sew them together by lacing wire through the holes in the hardware cloth. Hardware cloth is nasty to work with so perhaps your husband could be persuaded to help, or possibly a neighborhood hardware store would make a cone.

Pack Sphagnum moss firmly into the cone. Then make a cover for the bottom of the cone to keep in the moss and to prevent the sharp edges of the hardware cloth from scratching the surface on which the tree will rest. Cut a circle of heavy cardboard slightly larger than the base of the cone and punch holes around the outside edge, about 1 inch apart. Lash the cardboard circle to the base of the cone with florist wire.

Gather together dozens of short flat-bottomed Pine cones that are new, hard and a pretty color, separating them by size. Starting at the bottom of the tree with the largest cones, position them around the base of the cone to be sure there are enough.

To fix each cone in place, both a 6-inch length of #24 florist wire and a pre-wired wooden florist pick will be needed. First wrap the 6-inch length of wire around the base of the cone and twist together firmly, leaving a 2-inch "tail." Next take the wire attached to the pick and wrap it around the base of the cone. Twist the pick and the "tail" together tightly until the pick is firmly fixed at a 90° angle to the bottom of the cone.

Remove the top from a bottle of white craft glue and insert the wooden pick into the glue. Immediately stick the pick through one of the holes in the hardware cloth and push it all the way into the moss. Place the second cone next to the first in the same way, fitting it so tightly next to the first that their scales are meshed. Continue this procedure all the way around.

Begin the next row by fitting the first Pine cone into a spot between two cones in the bottom row. Determine which hole the wooden pick will enter before inserting it into the glue. Go round and round, the cones diminishing in size as you work up the cone, until the hardware cloth base is completely covered. Choose small cones for the very pointy top of the tree. The tiniest cones of all make good fillers glued into the bare spaces where the wired-in cones do not fit together tightly.

When the entire tree is completely covered, spray it thoroughly with clear lacquer several times to make it sparkle and to protect it from dust and dirt. Store the Pine cone tree under plastic wrapping when not in use.

This decoration may be displayed just as it is on a bed of greens, or it could be surrounded by a green wreath. The tree acquires more style, however, if it is placed on a low compote.

For my grandchildren I have studded the little trees with tiny carved wooden figures imported from Germany, Switzerland and Spain. (This makes an expensive tree.) They are wired and put into place with glue in the same way as the Pine cones.

The tree may also be trimmed with red velvet bows, or small artificial fruit. Choose decorations that will last, but try to avoid ceramics because they break so easily. You may want to crown the tree with an attractive small angel.

# A Honey Protea Wreath

*Designed By Mrs. Paul Dibrell Sowell*

## Materials:

Thirty-six inch length of 6-ply wire

#24 florist wire

Brown floral tape

6 yards of 1 1/4-inch brown velvet
    ribbon

Fourteen dried Honey Proteas, *Protea*
    *mellifera*

Ten small bell-shaped Eucalyptus
    pods

Eighty-one White Pine cone scales

Eleven Pecans

## Tools:

Electric hand-held drill with #2 bit
to make holes in Proteas and Eucalyptus pods.

Large darning needle to make holes
in White Pine cone scales.

Block of wood to be used as a holding device when making holes in
flowers, pods or scales with either
the drill or the needle.

Small pair of pliers used to pinch a
hanger in the 6-ply wire wreath
frame. Use them again to wrap the
unravelled wire ends of the 6-ply
wire tightly around the wreath ring.
Pliers will also be helpful to secure
the wire stems of the decorations
tightly around the wreath frame so
they will not slip out of place and to
prevent loose wire ends from pierc-
ing skin.

Since these wreaths take so very
long to make, the discovery that
most of them I have produced hang
in permanent settings has been very
satisfying to me. Indeed, although I
began to make them originally for
our Christmas Sale, they really are
not especially seasonal and it does
seem that anything upon which so
much time and effort is lavished
should be enjoyed more than two or
three weeks of the year.

The aim of this design is to create
a wreath with a feeling of openness.
For that reason it is built on a wire
ring with the top 8 inches left bare
to accommodate the bow. Every
item on the wreath has its own
stem.

Prepare a 12-inch wreath ring by
using a 36-inch length of 6-ply wire.
Unravel 3 inches at each end of the
wire and form a hanger by pinching
a loop a few inches in from one of
the unravelled ends. Now shape a
12-inch circle by lapping the wire
around twice until the unravelled
ends are on opposite sides of the
hanger. Carefully twist the unravelled ends around the wreath ring.
Make them as flat and smooth as
possible.

Wrap the entire circle and the
loop with brown floral tape.

Honey Protea are available from florist supply shops, where they can be found in bunches of hard, flat, dried brown flowers, 1 1/2 to 2 1/2 inches in diameter, fixed on stiff wire stems. Remove the wires and drill a hole, if necessary, across the base of each flower with a #2 bit. Insert an 8-inch length of #24 florist wire through the hole, and twist it together. Wrap a length of brown tape around the base of the flower and down the wire. First smear a little glue on the bottom of the flower to be sure the tape will hold. Prepare fourteen Honey Proteas in this manner. The glue will need to dry before you can begin to use them on the wreath.

Each of the ten Eucalyptus pods will also need to have a hole drilled across its base, be wired and wrapped around the base and down the stem with tape. A little glue will be helpful here, too.

To prepare the 81 White Pine cone scales, first pull them from the stems of several large White Pine cones, using only unblemished scales of bright color. With a sharp darning needle make a hole 1/4 inch from the base of each scale. Insert a 7-inch wire through the hole and twist it around the scale so that it holds the scale upright on the wire. Smear some glue on the scale and then wrap brown floral tape around the bottom of the scale and down the wire.

Eleven Pecans will each need to be drilled across the end and wired with an 8-inch wire stem. Brown floral tape should begin a third of the way up the side of the nut before it starts down the stem. Again, use glue to make sure the tape will stay in place.

Begin to make the wreath by creating a focal point of clustered Pecans exactly opposite from the hanger. Arrange the Pecans to look like Grapes with nine nuts hanging outside the ring and two Pecans on the inside of the ring pointing up. The two largest Proteas should be wired in place to cover the center of the Pecan cluster. Twist three stemmed White Pine cone scales together and attach them to the wreath ring so they appear to be coming out from behind the center top of the cluster of nuts. Two more groups of three wired scales complete the focal point by coming from behind the Pecans on either side at the bottom.

The remainder of the wreath is built upward from the focal point. Because each side should be exactly alike, the order in which the material is wired onto the wreath will be given for one side only. It is best to bring both sides up together rather than doing all of one side first. Remember to leave 4 inches bare at the top on both sides.

As a general rule, the Proteas are wired over the center of the ring and all the other material should appear to be coming out from behind the flowers to one side or the other. Because each item is wired individually, there will be some leeway for pushing them into position, but nothing on the wreath should be floppy.

1) Immediately beyond the focal point wire a group of three stemmed scales to the outside.
2) A Honey Protea
3) Three stemmed scales to the inside
4) A Honey Protea
5) Three clusters of three stemmed scales, nine altogether, to outside
6) Three Eucalyptus to inside
7) A Honey Protea
8) Three scales to outside
9) A second cluster of three scales to the outside
10) Three scales to inside
11) A Honey Protea
12) Six scales to outside
13) One Eucalyptus pod to inside
14) A Honey Protea
15) Three scales, one to inside, two to outside
16) A Honey Protea
17) One Eucalyptus pod to outside
18) Three scales, one inside, one center, one outside.

Spray the completed wreath three times with triple-thick clear spray. Allow at least five hours between sprayings.

Using 1 1/4-inch wide brown velvet ribbon wrap the entire wreath frame, carefully weaving around the wires. Be sure to wrap the hanger and make certain the ribbon is tight. Glue it down where it ends in back.

Make a bow of the same ribbon, large and full enough to cover the 8 inches at the top of the wreath that were left bare.

Though the instructions given here are quite specific, a similar wreath can be made with fewer Proteas. If flowers of varying sizes cannot be found, the same size flowers can be used throughout the wreath. In place of the dried Honey Protea flowers, the wreath could feature the tips of Deodar Cedar cones. If these cones are used, fuzzy wire pipe cleaners must be glued into holes drilled in the core of the cone, making them look like lollipop sticks. The pipe cleaners should be wrapped with brown floral tape, secured with glue.

Instead of Eucalyptus pods, or in addition to them, Beach nut burrs can be used. These are wired across the top so their wires must be wrapped with brown floral tape before they are attached.

Whatever materials are used, everything should be wired firmly in place and nothing should droop.

# Index to Instructions

(Index to instructions, continued)

# SOURCES OF SUPPLY

**Brown Seed Company**
P.O. Box 1792
Vancouver, WA 98668
Free catalog, $25 minimum order
Wholesale quantities

**The Flower Designer's Bench**
P.O. Box 839 - 141 Dunning Avenue
Auburn, NY 13021
Catalog free on request

**Gloria's Cone Tree**
245 North Third
Jefferson, OR 97352
Catalog $2. refundable with order

**The Pine Cone Shop**
Route 2
Park Rapids, MN 56470
Free price list

**Western Tree Cones**
P.O. Box 1418
Corvallis, OR 97339
Catalog $1

*Typesetting by*
*Art Comp and Design Company*
*Timonium, Maryland*
*Typeface — Andover*
*Text — 11/13*
*Headings — 38 point*
*Italics — 10/11*

*Printing and Binding by*
*The John D. Lucas Printing Company*
*Baltimore, Maryland*
*Offset lithography*

*Book design by Ellen Oliver Parsons*

*Printed in U.S.A.*